WILD ONES

LIONS

by JILL ANDERSON

NorthWord®
Minnetonka, Minnesota

On the plains of Africa, two small golden cats pounce and play in the tall grass.

These cats are not pets. They are young lion cubs!

They are
practicing
moves that
will help them
become good
hunters someday.

Lion cubs grow up under the careful watch of their mothers, aunts, and female cousins.

These females, or lionesses, make up a group called a pride.

Lionesses like to stick together.

They hunt for food as a group. They use their big, pink tongues to clean each other. They even let other lions' cubs have a drink of their milk.

A few adult males live with the pride.

Their long, bushy manes make them easy to spot. A male's job is to guard the pride's territory so his cubs can grow up safely.

This is important, because when a cub is first born, it is helpless. It can't see or walk. A mother lion keeps her newborns in a hidden den until they are ready to join the pride.

The pride spends most of its time snoozing in the grass.

In the heat of the day, the big cats
may stretch out on a hilltop or a
tree branch to catch a cool breeze.

The lions are storing up all their energy for the nighttime hunt. As day turns to evening, they **s-t-r-e-t-c-h** and greet each other by rubbing heads.

The playful cubs chase anything that moves.

In the fading light,
the male lions
roar
to tell other males to
stay away.
Both males and females
roar to keep in touch
with the pride.

Lions have no trouble finding antelope and other prey in the dark.

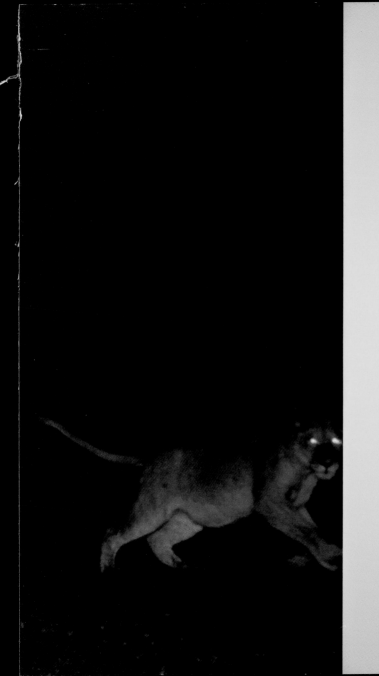

They
sneak up
until they are

close enough to

Everyone

shares the

big meal.

With full bellies, the lions greet the sunrise.

It's time for the sleepy cats to settle down for a long, lazy nap.

For Felix

—J. A.

Composed in the United States of America
Designed by Lois A. Rainwater • Edited by Kristen McCurry

Text © 2006 by Jill Anderson

NORTHWORD
Books for Young Readers
11571 K-Tel Drive
Minnetonka, MN 55343
www.tnkidsbooks.com

Photographs © 2006 provided by:
Digital Vision: cover, back cover, pp. 1, 4, 5, 9, 17, 24; Yva Momatiuk/John Eastcott/Minden Pictures: pp. 2-3;
Mitsuaki Iwago/Minden Pictures: pp. 6, 7, 12-13, 20-21; Frans Lanting/Minden Pictures: pp. 8, 14, 15, 21, 22-23;
Shin Yoshino/Minden Pictures: p. 16; James Gritz/Alamy: p. 11; JupiterImages Corporation: p. 18.

Library of Congress Cataloging-in-Publication Data

Anderson, Jill.
Lions / by Jill Anderson.
p. cm. -- (Wild ones)
ISBN 1-55971-952-4 (hardcover) -- ISBN 1-55971-953-2 (softcover)
1. Lions--Juvenile literature. I. Title.

QL737.C23A55 2006

599.757--dc22

2005038018

Printed in Singapore
10 9 8 7 6 5 4 3 2 1